A BOOK OF POETRY

THE BEHIND

PAINED MASK

KHALID IBN ANDERSON

THE BEHIND

KHALID IBN ANDERSON

A BOOK OF POETRY

THE BEHIND: PAINED MASK

KHALID IBN ANDERSON

A BOOK OF POETRY

LAZY GAL SWOFIYAH SELF PUBLISHING &
THINGS LLC

This book is a collection of poems written over the years. A collection of thoughts from the recess of my mind that I allow to fly regardless of my stationery position.

Copyright © 2025 by KHALIB IBN ANDERSON
THE BEHIND: PAINED MASK

Cover art by Khalid Ibn Anderson
Cover design by Tanya Chambers of IGSS-P&T LLC
Editing: Lazy Gal Swofiyah Self-Publishing & Things LLC

This book is the paperback edition of THE BEHIND: PAINED MASK, published by LAZY GAL SWOFIYAH SELF-PUBLISHING
THINGS LLC
Rochester, NY 14609

Published and printed in the United States Of America

LAZY GAL SWOFIYAH SELF-PUBLISHING & THINGS LLC
https://www.lazygalswofiyahself-publishingthingsllc.com

Library of Congress Control Number: 2025913336

ISBN: 979-8-9989798-5-9

DEDICATION

My wife, my fire, so much could be said, so much should be said. The best of all I could ever say is, "May all your Dreams and Desires be fulfilled in this life and the next. Ameen"

To all those who were out there for me, I thank you.

To those who gave me the nourishment needed to stand up and survive every and all elements: Kevin Louis Anderson, Julia Mae Davis, Juliette Elizabeth Anderson, Nora Lucille Davis, Barbara J. Mc Cullough, Richard Sylvester Anderson, Jacqueline Knowlin, Patricia Knowlin, Denise Knowlin, Ervin Smalls, Sr., Gerald Fabien Anderson, Sr., Mark Anthony Anderson, Frances Ann Smalls, Delaine Cook-Green.

I thank you all.

Prologue

The distinguished and revered title of a true warrior can be bestowed upon anyone who has bravely engaged in the harrowing and often traumatic experiences of a war! It is a prestigious honor granted to all those valiant individuals who have steadfastly refused to yield to the basic, yet overwhelmingly powerful emotions of grief, anxiety, regret, depression, or jealousy that so frequently accompany such formidable trials. During this arduous and punishing battle, as well as all others, war paint is worn in the form of a resilient mask, symbolizing unwavering strength and enduring perseverance.

Take this intriguing journey THE BEHIND: PAINED MASK and peer deeply into the heart and mind of a war-torn warrior who resolutely refused to succumb to the apparent doom and despair that threatened to engulf him at every turn.

TABLE OF CONTENT

Chapter 1

PLEASE HEAR ME

A love constructed around many boundaries, a love you have not accepted with ease. Eyes closed you cannot see the light, and that causes me endless sleepless nights. Tears in my eyes, as my pain destroys my insides.

Love and affection, no way to get your attention.

I made many attempts and perhaps a mistake, but my trust, my love, my dedication was never fake. Someone's focus simply misplaced.

Trust the heart as you reminisce on it all, from the very first call. The early soft spoken words which was loudly heard, intellectual conversations, love delivered without reservations.

Remember, do you remember all we have

been through, then you will know my heart belongs to you.

Stop fighting and you will see, bow down and give me! The connecting piece, a sweet humble wife.

Chapter 2
YOU ARE NOT MISSING ANYTHING

This is the cry of those who lie because they want to comfort your pain inside. I truly appreciate the sympathy, although you must agree that the truth can be found in reality.

My child has reached one, two, fifteen, eighteen, what do you mean. His first trip to school, giving her the first golden rule. Assisting with tying their shoes, oh Lord the first time they fell and wept, or the simple pleasure of watching over them while they slept.

You are not missing anything cannot take away from the sting, of sleeping in prison instead of the comfort of my bed.

The warmth of my wife in the dark or the joy of walking in the park.

Family reunions and cookouts, stop playing

before I pronounce the many aspects that make me denounce that concept that you are not missing anything. Do not make me tell you the songs that a convict sings. So instead of making that statement: "You are not missing anything" ask that question: **"Can I do anything?"**

WHO CRIES?

Chapter 3

WHO CRIES IN THE JUNGLE WHEN A SOUL IS LOST TO THE STRUGGLE

Word? You serious? Damn! Yo, what's for chow? Stop! Are we that delirious? In the same breath of death, we spare a second of reflection because a minute is too long, the next video is on, or the yard run has begun.

What have we turned into? The clones of data, our emotions in the mode of stealth, under the radar concealed from view, make no mistake this could be you.

Damn you don't say? The homie passed away, yo what you doing, arms or chest? Naw I'm hitting that bar for 20 sets you heard, then I'm coming back to blaze that box of b-dird.

You talking about Ak the good brother? On the movement! Remember it's just another day when a convict passes away.

Unless you stop and say: "His life is equal to mine. He deserves to shine" and through me he can if I take the proper stand. Because a soul is not forgotten unless it is forgotten and I will never forget cause one day it could be I and I'm not looking for anyone to cry, but I will wonder who cared enough to pause and say goodbye.

Chapter 4
THE TORTURE OF THE RING

The torture of the ring is like being tied up and forced to withstand the bites of a thousand mosquito stings an irresistible itch that makes you feel like screaming on a bitch!

But who would I be if I placed the blame of my self-inflicted pain on anyone besides me?

Who would I be if I went out of my way to share my misery?

That same no good for nothing son who started this bid on the eve of 1991.

No! I worked too hard to be a man of honor and dignity. Get off your spoiled behind I say and put that bull in the trash today.

Give in to some self-investment and make sure this time is well spent. I have to keep the focus on me if I truly want stability.

Chapter 5
IN MY DREAMS

In my dreams everything is so much better, even the rain is sweeter; and the snow that falls is fun for all.

In my dreams we all are free, come look into my dreams and see what I see. No problems for starters, no need for martyrs.

We will learn to play without the pressure of peers getting in the way, causing us to sway from our true desire. Leaving us to wither in the fire of doubt and confusion too live in a world of illusion.

In my dreams freedom is an amusement enjoyed by all. Do you see what I see, the power created for you and me? The power to laugh, the power to say I can, the power to say I am.

A RESTLESS
SOUL

Chapter 6
A RESTLESS SOUL

A restless soul looking into all it was told
about the survival skill, as it battles day to day
in a hell that is all too real.

Yet unknown to the average soul, who has
never lived in a world so cold.

Emotions mixed in conflict, so hard to see the
way when your vision is sick.

Plagued by the extreme illnesses of hatred and
shame, with only self to blame.

A restless soul attempting to be bold, with an
outstretched head under the oppressor's blade.
Can a life lived in irony, die with dignity?

Chapter 7

SURVIVAL

Survival is a word many use, yet only a few I know understand it. I know there are many more that do and I pray Allah helps all of us that do and may those who don't know, never know.

In the true face of survival everything becomes a threat, the natural elements become something to fear.

Naked in a world with no shelter from the wing, rain, heat or cold. Light and darkness, closeness and loneliness presents a threat.

Until you have been stranded alive with no life, you would never truly know the fear of the natural elements or the true sense of survival. Hopefully you never will.

Chapter 8
REFLECTIONS

I live in a world of corruption and deceptions, watching the news daily viewing constant revelations.

Different scenes and faces yet the same situations.

It hurts to be around people with such a distorted view and twisted perceptions.

Yet, who am I? What can I do to bring forth the proper corrections?

I am so frustrated and tired. Still, I continue to fight and remain focused in the right direction.

Chapter 9
SHIT AIN'T ALWAYS FUNNY

Shit ain't always funny when you are living your life as a crash test dummy, going from wall to wall with no vision, guided by the non-existence of a mother or father, like Nathan McCall makes you want to holler.

Shit ain't always funny as you run around chasing cash, wearing a mask of illusion and confusion. Masquerading as a man without a plan. Responsibility? What is that silly a word heard yet unknown to a groan.

Shit ain't always funny when my peers call me money and my clothes are from thrift shops and the Salvation Army. Sneakers leaning like the Eiffel Tower, Shh, while I run up on this fool and snatch him by the collar. As I hit him in the head you check his pockets for them dollars.

Shit ain't always funny when all I craved was love, peace, and happiness. Yet the dish I was served was a shitty mess.

If I Knew Then What I
Know Now

Chapter 10
IF I KNEW THEN WHAT I KNOW NOW

If I knew then what I know now would I be responsible or still live foul? Would I peddle the mountain to work or still peddle that dirt?

If I knew then what I know now would I trade in the Heinekens for paper and pens? Marching to Franklin, instead of running after those Benjamin's? Would I continue to be the fool or would I play by the rules?

If I knew then what I know now could I change anything? Would I still cause pain or would it be love I bring? Would I continue to live selfishly or embrace my family needs as number one priority? Am I out of my mind because I believe my family is all of mankind?

If I knew then what I knew now would I be

the best father, son, and brother giving up my love of the streets that demanding above all others?

If I knew then what I knew now would I establish a life of structure, or would I still look for escape routes and excuses that lead to a destructive future?

Come Enter My World

Chapter 11
COME ENTER MY WORLD

Come enter my world where everything is
bleak, even to my family I am quite mystique.

All because of a long period of separation
held together by a thin line of communication.

That is stretched further with lies, what is the
true meaning of family ties?

When everyone cries and shouts I care, while
their actions make you sit wonder and stare.

Into the unknown darkness of your future,
hoping that in the end your family elevates to
your mental stature.

Giving birth to a memories family state,
bringing an end to this seemingly peril fate.

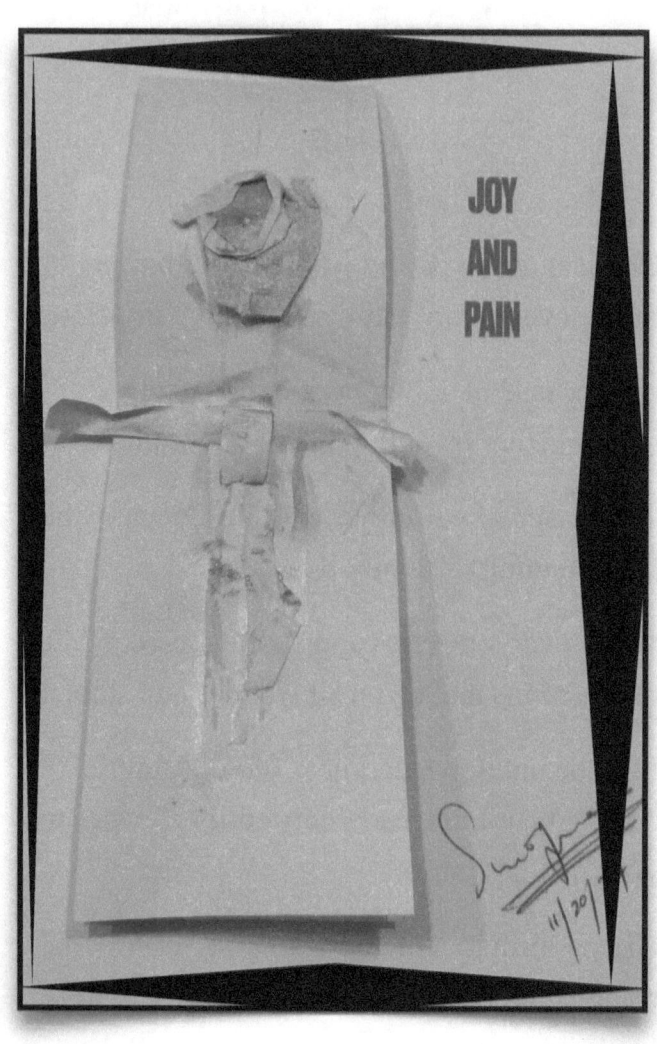

Chapter 12
JOY AND PAIN

Joy and pain there is a battle in my brain, as I fight to sustain.

A close comrade has achieved freedom, an accomplishment it is to face the hardships of a bid.

"Joy and pain, this confusion is insane?" I ask, happy for him no doubt. Still my heart cries for me, as it wonders when will it be that I can hug my family.

Who cares to understand, definitely not the man at the parole board with his continuous roar of two years. Tell me how can I really cheer?

Joy and pain, another momentous day I strive to maintain. Through tears I can see his happy face, while my heart beats at an unsteady pace.

I have to steady myself and keep my inspiration alive, even if I have to lean on a wall of lies.

Joy and pain I am alright, it is ok, I have my aim. I am just sick of this shit, locked with human misfits. Only counting on governmental statistics.

I am happy for you, I want you to achieve your every aim, it is just hard for me to truly celebrate as I battle with this joy and pain.

Caught Up And Spit Out

CHAPTER 13

CAUGHT UP AND SPIT OUT

A conceived coagulated blood clot, caught up in a womb and spit out. Into a confused misguided lost world without a father's love a child product of a height of fornication rejected from the first missed menstruation. Nine months of anger, hatred, no love when the head popped out, no breast in mouth. Pure Similac from the very first smack.

I cry, I scream, I shout, I have been caught up and spit out into a foul world without morals and guidance no doubt. Minds molded by sex, violence, drugs, racism, capitalism, marxism, and all other ism's and schisms that led you straight to prison. I have been caught up and spit out. Sold and told lies from dummies who play wise. Wake up and recognize before one dies. Should have listened to Gramps when she said stop it and watch it, instead I wanted to clock it and blow like a rocket.

Coming home with iced out chains looking brolic. Pure idolaters whose salvation is dead presidents buried in pockets. Caught up in a world of fallacies and fiction with bad diction. Empty refrigerators, while crack cooks in kitchen. Yes we have been caught up and spit out. Baby mamma drama, you working hard while she's steady bitch'en. I am not even going into all this damn snitch'en.

My Future will be unknown if I do not focus and establish my own. Because my past will never be forgot about, so I have to put forth action instead of just babbling my mouth. East against West, North against South why are we caught up and spit out?

Guns gangs and separations, long forgotten are the forty acres of reparations. We are caught up in fornications, soliloquist dictations of hate while pessimistic men use statistics as a basis for prolonged incarcerations. Teaching us lies through propaganda while unread is the miranda. Do you know children are starving to death in countries like Uganda? No, all we care about is Prada, Gucci and Dolce and Gabbana.

Decades have past and we are still caught up and spit out. Mental deficiencies are sufficient for those who prey on the weak, the lames and the meek. I am still striving for spiritual guidance regardless to what the news says about this and that priest.

Lost in the jungle of the stray path while the knowledge you seek is deep in self, but we are caught up in searching for wealth, not caring about our physical, spiritual, or mental health.

Many fought to be in the front, while the first place we run is to the back. Twisted is the facts that rappers lay down on tracks. Few get millions while millions of minds get twisted, mostly Latinos and Black.

But hey, I see you, my Caucasian brothers catching up in the degenerated race. Please do not forget your place, of being the raiser of our children in righteous ways, building foundations of what life is truly about cause if we do not, like us there will be caught up and spit out.

What can I say about life today? They say: **"If it is not rough it is not right."** As well they say: **"The key to success is to be able to maintain patience and be able to stand firm and persevere in the face of adversity."** I do believe in all of this.

What is my complaint? Yes, today I wish to complain and every day since November 1990. I have wished to complain and I do! I complain only to the Lord of the Universe, for it is He who has given man guidance to first know that He is real and not a myth. Thus after accepting that fact, one must adhere to the teachings. Why would you not when they are geared towards granting you success in this life and the next? Some would come up with many reasons, they also say: **"It is because they rather follow their forefathers**

even though they were clearly in error."

My mind says: **"It is easier to do wrong than stand for what is right and the reward for doing what is right are not always quickly evident. I do believe in time you will see the product of your actions whether right or wrong."** As the say: **"You shall receive what you strive for."** Still doing what is right times appears to be less promising. Is that why they say: **"The good guy finishes last?"**

What can I say about life today? I guess I am very tired. I refuse to lay down simply out of fear that I will not make it back up.

I want to live, I want to be successful and success to me is not defined by financial or materialistic gain.

I wonder what will become of me. A man who has spent the latter part of two decades locked in a living hell, a man who has cried all his tears away until now it is his heart that cries causing that precious life source to be drained.

Damn, is it all in vain?

DADDY'S QUEEN

CHAPTER 15
DADDY'S QUEEN

With precious thoughts of Daddy's Queen, I find myself still amazed that this is not a dream.

Looking at our photo I know from the glow of my rainbow that we will remain tomorrow, tomorrow, tomorrow, you know the flow.

Forever was decided from the very start, with one remark bringing us into the light and out of the dark.

You are my wife is what was said, seven months later we were wed.

Such a magnificent sight, dressed all in white, I know I looked to be in flight.

I was awe struck by the power of our Lord,

what have I done to afford such a great reward.

Years of struggle and sacrifice, all without a costly price.

All was done to establish who we are, you are my rainbow and I am your Star.

The joy we have given to each other is in constant bloom, against all odds and people's dreaded doom.

Within this time we have experienced many fears, does not your heart feel calmer with the passing of each New Year?

Each year brings in the commemoration of a blessed day, bringing us closer to the point we will be on our way.

Cruising down the highway to our home, Oh yes, I promise you will never feel alone.

Up under you is where I will be, content satisfied, truly complete.

CHAPTER 16
YOU NAME IT

This is not written because of a fleeting feeling.

This is etched with pain, as I realize I have lost my friend.

We had a love that overcame time and space, now it appears to hurt whenever we are face to face.

Is it because our love was so strong, that we cannot seem to get along?

Is it because of my silent strength that caused you to turn on your defense?

With your freestyle hello's void of emotions, did I not keep one promise of not creating or causing any commotions?

As you live your life as you pleased, was I not there as best as I could for your every need?

Is it because I did me that you finally realize shit stink, even though you rubbed your hands upon my face and never rinsed them in the sink.

You said I was strong, in this aspect you are wrong.

Evaluate more closely and you will see that I cannot handle it all, this is a physical, spiritual, and mental fall.

Short sweet and simple: **"To not have you as a friend, has definitely gotten under my skin."**

CHAPTER 17
WHAT WILL TOMORROW BRING

I sit in sorrow, wondering about tomorrow.

The pain of stress strangling me, grasping
wondering when I will be free.

What will become of me? It is the end of
2003.

Long past the eve of 1991, am I just an absent
father, long lost brother, a forgotten son?

I smother myself in grief, all this because of a
thief or was it truly me and my stupidity?

The careless thoughts of my son and unborn
daughter, my ignorance of being a father.

Thirteen years and one month has passed, and
I still feel like a total ass.

Fucked by my own hands, O' trust I am a
man, that is why I continue to stand.

This torturous penalty is just about done, I swear I will do my all to shine like the sun.

Raised up high in magnificence, showing myself and the world that this moment was well spent.

CHAPTER 18
NIGHTMARES

Have you ever had a nightmare of your daughter running after you as you giggle and fall? Or the terrible dream of being with your son tossing the football?

My soul still trembles over the one about taking my daughter to the mall, a tear has fell as I recall the one in which I observed my son grow tall.

My muscles tighten as I feel the pain race though me, from the horrible dream of cooking for my family.

I see Gramps, Mama Love, and Auntie "B", indeed in this dream I am free.

Everyone is laughing and having fun, there they go again the faces of my daughter and son.

Hey here comes their mothers, O' shit it's my brothers.

Yo! What's up? It has been a minute, it is all good because your time has ended.

Where's my sisters? There in the house, O God! As I open my mouth. Caught in a blank stare, trapped within this nightmare.

Of pleasant moans as me and my wife wrestle in bed, nightmares indeed when you are not home and you wake up in a prison's bed.

For
My
Sisters
In
The
Struggle

CHAPTER 19

FOR MY SISTERS IN THE STRUGGLE

Who cares to understand, the struggle of a single parent woman?

Do not look for the governmental statistic, they do not supply the need for the emotional sick.

All they do is garner the fuel from the absent fool.

Who cares to relate to the debate, "Can a woman properly teach a boy to become a man?" Definitely not anyone who refused to take a stand and hold the hand of his precious little man.

Who cares that I am raging through the pages, searching for ages for a cure to eliminate this fatherlessness that is quite contagious.

I say who cares about this loneliness, dripping

stress upon my dress as I starve for the caress of a firm hand upon my breast. No! Do not say I am a mess because I confess.

I just want to know who cares.

Please say no more, your cry is like a lions roar sending chills to the roots of my heart!

Now allow me to tie my boots and began to start to be the responsible man that plays his part within the family structure, leading you all into a confident future.

Lady just never forget as I stabilize my throne, you are not alone. By my side allow me to guide with knowledge and wisdom that developed through many tears over a lot of lost years.

Who Cares To Know

CHAPTER 20
WHO CARES TO KNOW

Woman say they exhale when they recognize their relationship has went stale.

At the point when they are no longer caught in a blue funk, and they can embrace a bottle of wine and perhaps a joint.

They call on girl friends to celebrate, the theme being: **"Free the dome of hate."**

A cathartic experience of the mind, cleansing the way for a bright sign.

Who cares to know, that a man cannot glow until he establishes a friend within his woman and not a foe.

A man exhales on his wedding night, nervous impressions all take flight.

A man can never rest or be at peace, let alone

be complete until he finds joy in the presence of his wife.

STOLEN INNOCENCE

CHAPTER 21
STOLEN INNOCENCE

It all started with a kiss and ended with a dismiss.

Why did you take a precious moment of father and daughter, elevating it so much farther.

Farther than my mind could ever conceive. On bending knees I cry please, please explain this to me. Give my heart ease.

Our innocence you stole, I have to ask:
"What was your goal?"

As you fixed your face to conjure up an image of malice and disgrace.

I fought hard to keep my head held high, although deep inside all I could do was cry, sigh and wish I would disappear or run and hide.

Today I know there is no place safe from the devil's face. No place to hide from jealousy, hatred, and pride.

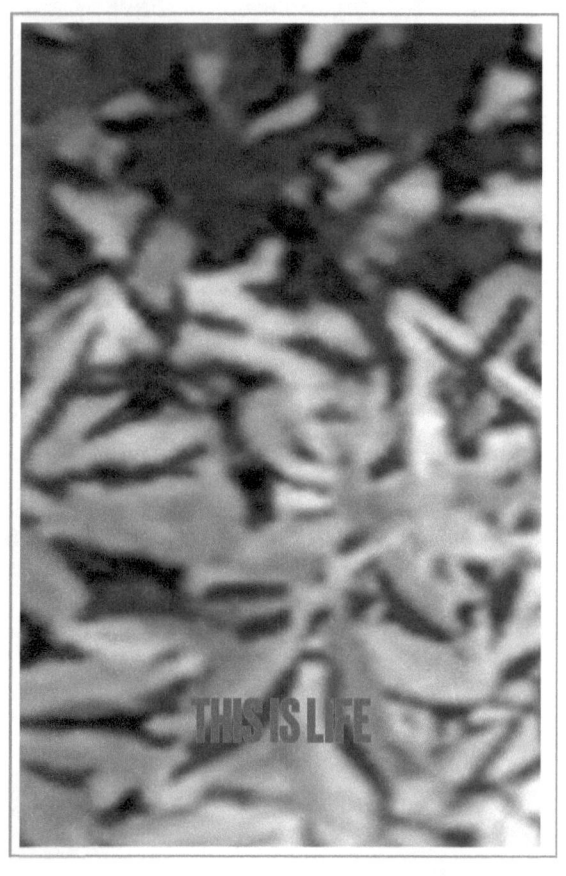

CHAPTER 22
THIS IS LIFE

Loneliness, regrets. A life that is a mess.

Caused by my own hands, does that make me less than a man?

I come to you to release my mind, fore only you took the time to understand, to show concern and give inspiration.

Elevating me out of my destructive situation.

Making me realize that a fall is not all it appears to be, that life goes on and dreams can be a reality. All I have to do is believe in me.

Doubts and fears are not an illusion, I just have to cut them free to escape the confusion.

Life goes on and dreams come true, you tell me time and time again: "The power to stand lies within".

You have to understand that pure fruits of happiness I have not tasted in years, everything has been bittersweet, tainted through tears.

I hear your voice of encouragement, life goes on and dreams come true, do today what you have to do.

Clear your voice, hopes your scope, set your sight, and with all you're might, accept the obstacles because this is life.

One Call Is All It Took

CHAPTER 23
ONE CALL IS ALL IT TOOK

One call is all it took to make me take a deep look at the meaning of the word father, lo and behold the closer I looked my image became farther and farther.

I feel so ashamed to hear another man call my baby "Pooka," a nickname that says I am here, as it is full of comfort and care.

Pooka, Pooka he calls as I listen to your footsteps coming down the halls.

For a second you pause as you alert him that dinner is ready, prepared by your own hand, man! How much more can I stand?

My daughter has prepared her first plate, should I hang up and retreat? Surely what I am hearing is a family complete.

My intrusion cannot be a welcomed one,

tolerated as a joke on you very little fun.

I have not called subsequently, because mentally I am unprepared, confused and scared of the harsh reality that through my ignorance and immaturity I lost the most precious gift that can be given to humanity.

I fought hard to compete. Sending money, gifts and an occasional treat.

Helping with school books and school cloths, O' Allah knows I do these things with joy as I cannot ignore that I fall very short with assisting with the real pleasure of guiding and comforting your delicate heart.

Yes, Father and Father from the mark I fall. Waiting on one call: **"Daddy wake up, wake up daddy."**

Believe me, one call can change it all.

Be True To Self

CHAPTER 24
BE TRUE TO SELF

Around my boys the thug I reveal but the man I hide. Not realizing that we are all doing the same thing, keeping it inside.

Some of us grab street names to describe who we are, a misconception and false image that does not define us by far.

No one in the streets wants to feel un-excepted, so they stand their ground, doing what is expected.

Grown men using Hip Hop phrases, not realizing how stupid they sound. Over thirty years old walking around saying you heard, I keep it real my G, Yo son that's my word.

Now do not get me wrong I am not trying to down play ebonics, but if you're over thirty years old and still using those phrases you need to get hooked on phonics.

You're not changing with time, you're letting

time change you. While you need to know when you reach a certain age changing is what you do.

I believe woman love thugs because of what they see, a bunch of grown men trying to imitate what they watch on TV.

I am stepping away from the crowd, a man is what I represent. I am not afraid to let anyone know I pray to Allah every day I repent.

I love slow music, laying back, writing music and poems. If I cannot be accepted for who I am than I rather be alone.

CHAPTER 25
STAND UP

I could stand on the corner and pitch all day, does that make me a man, or am I letting society make me believe that I am doing all I can.

Do I have scar face dreams of living the life as the self-proclaimed King Of The World, but when faced with racketeering or king pin charges will I be able to walk the walk or perform my best twirl.

Is it worth trying to keep up with the Jones, has Hip Hop took over my life? Is Bitch a word I put in my vocabulary that best describes my mother, sister or wife.

Newport slogan: **"Is alive with pleasure"** but on the box it clearly tells you that you can catch cancer.

Do you really want a pleasure that can cut
your life short, if not then do not take that
next drag on that Newport?

Am I a father for being a part of their lives,
and never found myself in court, am I wrong
for not wanting to refer to my Black Sisters as
birds and chicken heads. Am I considered a
square because in my life shivery is not dead.

I am my own man, no Hip Hop or street
Codes will determine who I am, I am a
Servant of Allah, I provide for my family, and
for righteousness I stand.

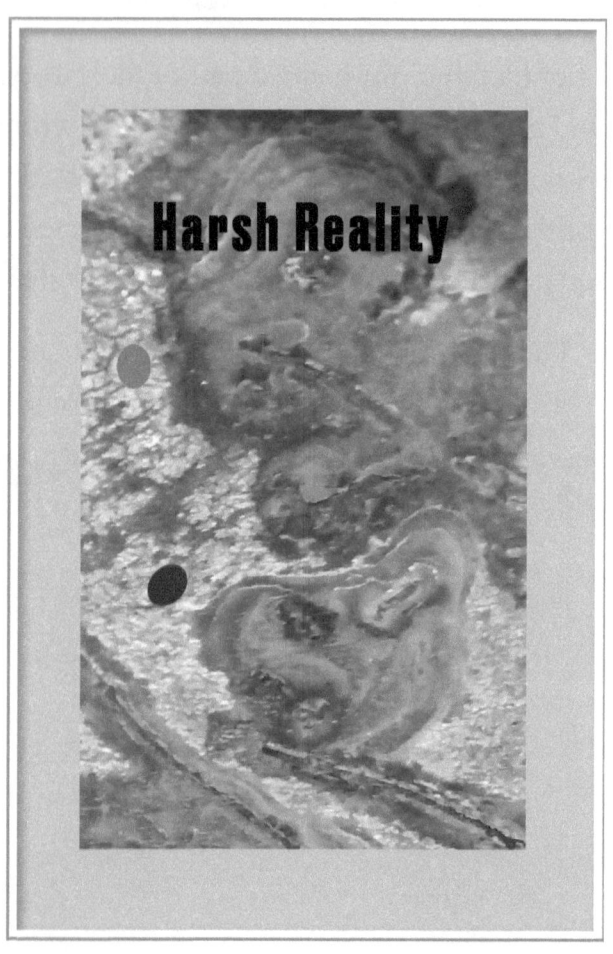

Harsh Reality

I had a nightmare that my love came to an end, after seven years I have lost my best friend.

I watched a man in my house putting my child to sleep, I tried to scream but I could not speak.

I thought I was dead because my presence was not known, I could visibly see that my house was no longer my home.

So I sat on the sofa to observe everything, I saw my love was no longer wearing my ring, she openly pranced around the house, happy as can be, she even began to sing. But who was making her happy was not me.

I felt a sharp pain in my heart, so I clenched my chest, and asked Allah how did this mess start?

I hoped off the sofa, and fell to my knees, and said Allah I am begging you please. Please take away this pain, and all that I see, this is my family, and this cannot be.

All of a sudden I opened my eyes, and I was back in my bed, in Orleans Correctional Facility with sweat pouring from my head.

The C.O. called my name for mail, I ran to get it, because the woman I love was reaching out, giving apart of herself to me, easing and erasing this harsh reality.

CHAPTER 27
INTROSPECTION

After carefully viewing him over, I see we possess some of the same characteristics which should have drew us closer, yet it only created closure.

Two different sculptures of the same stone, seeing in two totally different visions, yet it appears that he could be my clone.

Eye to eye we connect, the glare that he is giving me says: **"That man will never fold as long as he is living he commands respect."**

Despite my ego we are sharing the same fascination, dividing the same motive I know there is something missing upon gazing, something truly amazing in this situation.

While analyzing I see his attire met my

expectation his taste is similar to mine, even his movements match my very move as if he is reading my mind.

Is he mocking my actions? ? Perhaps he can be asking the same questions.

I wonder what his purpose for existing is. Is his instincts for survival? Is he moral-less? Can he possibly be my rival?

He looks so familiar and this intensifies a little friction. Not able to set time or place creates some dissension.

Never to prove me wrong my senses do not differ, so smoothly I distance myself and he repeats the same gesture.

Never breaking his stare, I am starting to feel little pressured and scared.

Immediately my judgements scream caution, so I test him by giving him another inch. True to himself he gives the same motion.

Now I am less scared and more frustrated so I contemplate an approach, unaware that this is his very hope.

So cautiously I watch the eyes that are watching me and I see in retrospect, the inner soul that I must protect.

TORMENTED
THOUGHTS

CHAPTER 28
TORMENTED THOUGHTS

What does this life hold for me? I often lay back and wonder, am I doomed to an existence of mediocrity filled with foul ups, bloops and blunders?

Spending most of my time in a US Prison System with the total of my existence and every decision plagued with a senseless ultimatum.

Wrecked with guilt of how I let those who believed in me down. Floating endlessly, sinking further in an ocean of peril I created for myself, causing me to drown.

Haunted by the ghost of past opportunities I made no attempt to seize, vividly recounted mistakes, bad decisions and failures that have affected this seemingly meaningless existence I call life to various degrees.

Do I have the capability to resurrect my thought, with the knowledge I sought?

To redefine my values and chart a course that will enable me to reach greatness, as I sail through these uncharted waters of this enigma I can only label a mess.

Is this my destiny, for me to be sentenced to living in a world of hell, tormented with could have's, should have's, what if's and I's until my eventual inevitable demise.

CHAPTER 29
I WILL

Coming face to face with the realization that I have G.O.D. given talents that enable me to become much more than I ever dared to dream, too aspire for.

I openly covet the embrace of change while my heart refuses to conform, so I analyze the necessary steps to endure the coming hardships that are sure to accompany the ghetto norm.

Readying myself to stay clear of my addictive penchant for the seemingly much easier wrong, enduring the degrading and dehumanizing treatment I suffered throughout my incarceration, intent on emerging strong.

Using the stress filled emotionally draining minutes that add up to years as fuel to empower me to reach the sky, compelling me to fight this bitterness and hatred that consumes me as every 1440 minutes go by.

Determined no matter how gloomy and gray things abide, not to let it extinguish my passion and fire that burns deep inside.

Failure is not an option nor anywhere near any destination I expect, my aspirations are: "Freedom, Love, Happiness, Success, simply a life lived honorably without regret.

A Woman's Worth

CHAPTER 30
A WOMAN'S WORTH

I have laid in my bed many nights trying to figure out a woman's worth, I have spoken to older brother's and went to the scripture for guidance in this search.

I prayed for help with this task, I learned I must first take off my mask.

In order to understand the worth of a woman you have to first be yourself, realizing that the riches of this land is the rib that was taken from man which holds his true wealth.

I thank Allah as I was no longer living in the blind, thy heart became very warm as beautiful thoughts began to fill my mind.

A woman is underrated at times and often not treated like the Queen she is, she is the back bone to our family's foundation, the nurture of our kids.

A woman is the Cream De La Cream, a beautiful painting on the wall, I am not just singling any one out, and I am talking about them all.

So I tip my hat to every woman that walks with grace on this earth, thank you for giving us the word priceless that is exactly your worth.

Searching With Eyes Closed

CHAPTER 31

SEARCHING WITH EYES CLOSED

Presidential debates, cause our pockets to deflate.

As the cost of living goes higher than we can reach, presidents constantly preach.

About tax cuts and aid for those in need, yet fueled by their own greed.

Created out of lust, conceived out of hate, so many times I question was I a mistake?

I cannot explain the evolution, yet I know the revolution.

Fully aware that the facts reflect we have a problem with mass destruction and corruption.

Sitting here in a cell staring directly at the floor wondering how I created hell.

In the penitentiary block on lock, with blue

and green cops, neither of which are made for shit.

Am I wrong for being mad? Is my soul wrong for being sad?

We allegedly live in a bureaucracy, labeled a Democracy, yet who really voted for each Presidency?

A democracy cannot be just when it elects officials to hold control over everybody.

I do not have anything against a righteous government, I just find it crazy that people have it hard to pay for medical treatment and rent.

Every word of the common people goes unheard.

Unplug your ears, listen to my fears. I am a changed man, do you not understand?

I never meant to cause tears and pain, I never meant to take away your sunshine, replacing it with rain.

Damn this time has torn us apart, still it is not enough to remove you from my heart.

Gone are the years, causing my eyes to blear with tears.

So I have to use my heart to guide me through this dark.

Eight in a week. Tell me how a parent can sleep, when their child cannot speak.

Tony, where have you been? I I Um. Shantay where are you going this time of night? I I Um.

I I Um is the sum of a lie to a parent who cannot rest because their nights are full of stress.

AM reports on CNN disclose last night's sin, or the local media brings the news to them as they are awaiting word from you.

A parent's nightmare is to stare into the glare of TV screens to find out what it means to lose a child to drugs, death or prison.

O' everyone knows there is no laughter when it comes to your daughter, caught in the grips. Being abused from the lips to the hips by a strange character called a pimp, who walks with a limp.

If you know what I am conveying, stop playing.

It is no longer about our children, by far.

The new cry is: **"Do you know where your parents are?"**

CHAPTER 33

INTERFERENCE

Here's your ring, because you did not tell me anything.

I had a right to know, you were putting on a show.

Was it the fear of rejection that created your web of deception?

Whether that fear lied within me or you, the right thing is what you were supposed to do.

It is a sin, to not stand for what you believe in.

My belief was in you and yours was in me, so how did you lay down knowing you had a family.

What pleasure can a moment bring, don't you know a true treasure is measured through meaning?

Your clarity will come when you end it, as you contemplate your life and how wisely you spent it.

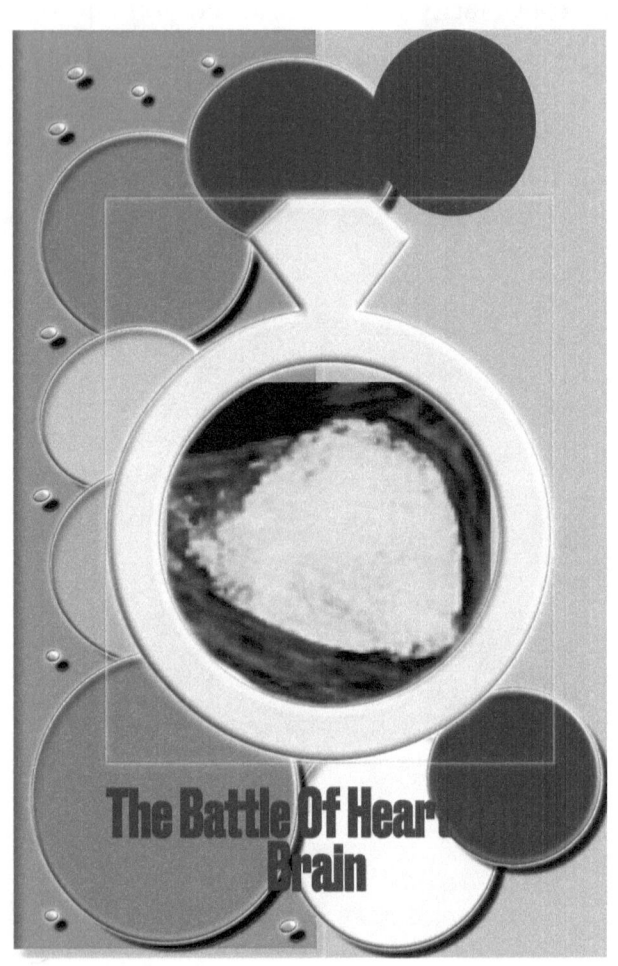

The Battle Of Heart & Brain

CHAPTER 34

THE BATTLE OF HEART AND BRAIN

What am I doing? Why do I continue to garner you within my heart, holding on to visions of you and I.

Could the answer be that I am just emotionally imbalanced, living in a world that's even more unbalanced?

I do know that from time to time I have visions and fantasies that are far from reality and talking with you gives these images fuel as it is always a thrill; more so a treat so to speak that is not always readily available and when it is I savior it.

The forbidden fruit! Why am I still lusting and craving for what I know I cannot have?

I do not think I should be writing you this type of letter, but I must because year after year I have fought to contain these feelings. My heart and mind has battled. My heart has a burning desire to bring forth its content and my heart says: **"The only way I can become free is through you or with you."**

My mind is very challenging and it questions the worth of bringing such delicate details to light? My mind also says: **"See things for what they are, for what they have been, move on and create a new life."**

I have always loved having you in my life. You never left my life because I always kept you near. Throughout the years I felt your love and I know you felt mine. Our love has continued to grow in its own way. Entwining and wrapping itself into a beautiful gift, too precious to open.

I realize that I am not going to be able to deal with my emotions until I am home and face to face with reality.

Reality. If you told me you do not dream of me in the manner that we are lovers, immersed within each other, my heart would be crushed as it has continuously been crushed!

Yes! Surprisingly there's still more room for it to be crushed, I've been told I have a big...

Reality. If you were to tell me that your arms are wide open welcoming me into them with love and commitment I would be overjoyed, and confused.

Yes! So many connecting strings would have to be harnessed or disconnected.

Perhaps I think too much, perhaps I want too much!

The Battle of my heart and mind continues.

I am smiling right now because I know the same way they...my heart and mind...worked together to produce this letter, they will work together ensuring that I make the right decision or giving me the strength to accept life's decision.

I love you and it may sound crazy, mentally

we never stopped being lovers. I know I have to wake up and stop dreaming. Get my act together and start living.

What I am going through and what I have to do in order to survive this madness is crazy!

I have to re shape my thinking and develop a new stance in many areas of my life.

When it comes to you, I felt you needed to know my dilemma of not knowing how to be your friend because I have only known and thought of you as my wife.

The Lie Of 1735

Who gave me the title African, Arabian, Caucasian, Dominican, Italian or Puerto Rican?

Is the answer simple or is it simply a diversion so I can forget who I really am.

A man unique in character and distinction, yet to think I am so different is truly fiction.

A man who blends into the melting pot of mankind like an exquisite meal, no need for racism, or separatism.

There, like a garlic clove, frustrating and sticky. To receive its benefit you must handle it harshly not gently.

Do not let anyone smother you by limiting your essence to any group, as a man belonging to the human race do not be duped.

We were created into many nations and tribes not to despise one another, yet to enjoy the flavor that comes from variety.

Too deny this is surely a casualty.

I love you all and I want you to love me, I will be patient because first you have to wake up, open your mind and see cognitively.

Then it will be acknowledged that we all are one race i.e. human, and your family is all of mankind!

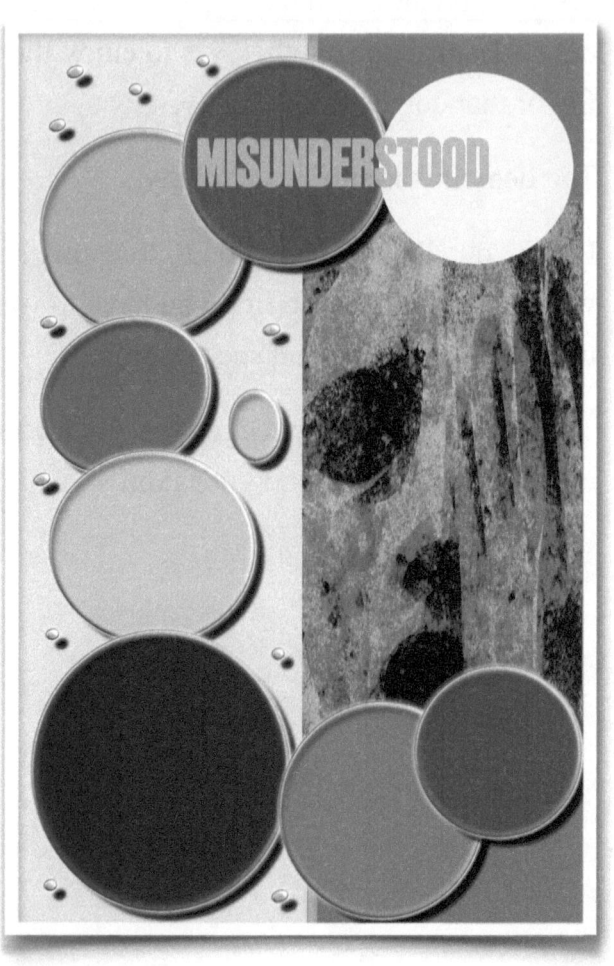

CHAPTER 36
MISUNDERSTOOD

Invest in me and you will see I am not that bad in fact I am good, just misunderstood like the majority of my brothers and sisters in what they labeled the hood.

A place where lies are hidden and government corruption is covered up, they promised us milk and honey but forced fed us a bunch of syrup.

That destroyed our molars i.e. mothers, our fangs i.e. fathers.

The strength of our communities that allowed us to eat, leaving us broken and beat to fend alone in the street.

With no proper name or identity, call me John Doe cause I have no history, everything I follow is fantasy or someone else's reality.

You say I should know better as you punish

me to the letter.

Knowing I had no direction because you systematically put road blocks in front of my education.

Highlighting fancy cars, platinum chains and shiny teeth, keeping me away from executive positions forcing us to fight to make ends meet.

We do not fight you, not because we are afraid, you are just never around, so in the hood it continues another brother faced down.

My point is be an individual, get up and take a stand because when you can reveal your true self then your being a real man.

SLEEPING GIANT

CHAPTER 37
SLEEPING GIANTS

Have you ever seen a sleeping giant?

One whose cognitive principle is I can't.

One who glamorizes self-hate and implanted that seed in his mate.

One who refuses his responsibility, because in his repose he cannot see.

Tell me, have you seen this character, I wish to alert him of his power.

Tell me, have you seen this character, I wish to enlighten him of his honor.

He's been in this coma state for way to long, this cycle must not go on.

Awaken mighty giant, no longer can you lay on your face being compliant.

Awaken mighty giant, awaken. You are

wanted by family and friends to bring this dilemma to an end.

A True Man

CHAPTER 38
A TRUE MAN

I am truly upset and I truly regret the game that men have played upon the opposite sex.

It is the sun's duty to shine upon the moon, so why were these lessons taught by fools.

Now the earth has degrees in hatred, jealousy and envy. Low self-esteem, animosity and hypocrisy.

Making me the recipient of their reciprocal ways, wishing they had better days.

So that the birth of our future would not be so obscure.

I want to free you from this state, stop you from being so obstinate.

Can you please give me your hand, trust in my plan, knowing that I can graciously honor you as the first gift giving to man.

Always Baby

CHAPTER 39
ALWAYS BABY

I want us to always look upon each other as best friends. Not just in mere words of expression, but in true affection.

I want us to always communicate our feelings openly, having no fear of rejection or the other's perception.

I want us to always melt in the presence of the other, having a bond that is so secure there's no need to smother.

I want us to always represent as a public role model, the perfect image to follow.

I want us to always cherish our marriage, as a memorial summer's night in Central Park with horse and carriage.

I want us to always remember the last will be first, so in our struggle to last we will never forget what "I do" birth.

I want us to always hold hands, so we'll stay connected as we venture to accomplish mine and your plans.

I want us to always create a love song, as our hearts beat and fingers creep all night long.

I want us to always stay focused on our Lord, fore it will be this consciousness that manifest our greatest reward.

If Walls Could Talk

CHAPTER 40
IF WALLS COULD TALK

If walls could talk, what would be their story to tell?

The Great Wall of China or The Great Wall of Berlin, would it be tells of laughter, torture or sin?

How about the walls that lined the many ships of the Middle Passage or the walls of Auschwitz and Nuremberg that witnessed the killing of masses.

The walls of the Oval Office, Pentagon, The Walls of Constitutional Hall that's long past gone.

Do you know the walls of Attica, Auburn, Bedford Hills, Clinton, Comstock or Coxsackie?

Prison walls that housed the worst of the worst and the best of the best.

Walls breath, sweat and I can only imagine how they have wept, because of all the secrets they have kept.

If walls could talk would we really want to listen?

Would it alter our perception or give conviction to our direction?

THE END

ACKNOWLEDGMENTS

"What good is a beautiful gift without the proper instructions for its effective utilization? What value does the precious gift of life hold if it is devoid of the essential gift of guidance? When you find yourself down on your back, the only sensible direction to look is up! I have endured an existence spent upon my back for many long years; yes, it has indeed been a time filled with overwhelming pain. Yet, despite this suffering, the beauty of life is still very much present. Gazing upwards, I can see beyond the layers of filth that life sometimes presents. One of the most wonderful sights I witnessed while lying on my back was none other than you, my beloved children. A multitude of emotions swirled within me as I beheld this vision, emotions so profound that I cannot even begin to explore their depths. At this moment, I wish for you to understand that what you have just finished perceiving was, and still is, a life fully lived. Within the grand tapestry of life, there are always two contrasting sides. Hot, cold; in, out; back or front.

Indeed, we have the capacity to move forward, choose your path wisely. Right or wrong, failure or success—these choices shape your destiny. The knowledge you need in order to make the right decisions is present all around you. This undeniable fact is what COMPELLED me to complete this important project for you, along with the understanding that you will need to navigate through all the complexities and nonsense that life will throw your way.

Another crucial pair to prepare for is: "facts and opinion." Strive to capture the truth through diligent study, speak the truth to maintain your energy steady, and surround yourself with individuals who share the same vision as you. Remember, eagles soar with eagles, while pigeons flock with pigeons. Learning to remain focused on what truly matters will help you in crafting a life that is, indeed, picture-perfect. Anyone who attempts to convince you that such a life is not possible simply does not belong on your team.

Tyrone, Jasmine, Khayson, Khalisa, Khalia we are one."

ABOUT THE AUTHOR

Khalid Ibn Anderson was born and raised in the City of Rochester, New York. He attended Frederick Douglass School, followed by Benjamin Franklin High School. The invaluable years spent in these educational institutions shaped his character, teaching him to be a strong, unapologetic male.

At the age of nineteen, he found himself in the New York State Correctional Facilities (NYSCF), where he remained until reaching the age of thirty-six. During this transformative period, he learned that life was truly what he made of it, gaining profound insights about his existence. It was in this reflective space that Khalid Ibn Anderson delved deep within himself to uncover the true meaning of life. He harnessed the knowledge gained from his extensive meditation practice and evolved into the accomplished writer he is today.

When he's not passionately immersed in writing, he enjoys indulging in the great outdoors, engaging in activities that ignite his spirit, such as fishing, hunting, cooking, or having meaningful conversations with others.

KHALID IBN ANDERSON
mr.khalidanderson@yahoo.com